The Seed Is in God's Word

Seed Principles to Overcome Life's Challenges

The Teaching Ministry of

Dr. E. L. Womack, Sr.

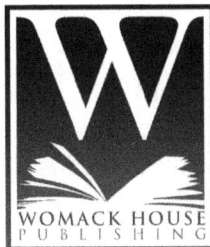

WOMACK HOUSE
PUBLISHING

Published in the United States of America

Scripture quotations marked KJV are taken from the King James Version.
Scripture quotations taken from the Amplified® Bible,
Copyright © 1954, 1958, 1962, 1964, 1965, 1987 by The Lockman Foundation. Used by permission. All rights reserved.
Scripture quotations from THE MESSAGE. Copyright © by Eugene H. Peterson 1993, 1994, 1995, 1996, 2000, 2001, 2002. Used by permission of Tyndale House Publishers, Inc. Used by permission. All rights reserved.

ISBN 978-0-9904219-0-0 (pbk)
LCCN 2014912728
For information about special discounts for bulk purchases contact Womack House Publishing, LLC.

Womack House Publishing, LLC
3965 East Brookstown Drive
Baton Rouge, LA 70805

womackhousepublishing@yahoo.com

(225) 357-1330

Contents

Dedication 4

Introduction 5

Chapter 1 – The Principle of the Seed 7

Chapter 2 – The Principle of Meditating on the Word 14

Chapter 3 – The Principle of Retaining the Word 19

Chapter 4 – The Principle of Watering the Seed 28

Chapter 5 – The Principle of the Seed at Work 34

Chapter 6 – The Principle of God's Ability in the Word . 41

Conclusion 51

Salvation Prayer 53

About the Author 54

Confessions 56

Dedication

I give honor and thanks to God the Father, the Son, and the Holy Spirit. He lives within me, teaches, and guides me. I heard His voice saying put this in a book: *"The Seed is in the Word."*

I want to dedicate this book to my beautiful wife, Audrey, who is the love of my life. She has been faithful and very supportive of me throughout this process.

I would like to also give thanks to all seven of my children, including my oldest, who has gone to be with the Lord.

Thanks to my grandchildren; I pray they continue to follow in God's steps.

Thanks to my sons-in-law for their faithfulness. Also thanks goes to Sharonne and Shawn for your help within the ministry. I love all of you for your encouraging words and support.

Dr. E.L. Womack, Sr.

Introduction

Many people are searching for quick fix answers to life's situations, but the answer can only be found in the word of God, which is the seed. The majority of people do not want to wait for the answers to be revealed to them, and their quick fix answers are not always what they expect. The Bible gives the best solution to every situation. John 5:39 Amplified version says, "You search and investigate and pore over the Scriptures diligently, because you suppose and trust that you have eternal life through them. And these [very Scriptures] testify about Me!" The believer has his or her life mapped out for them if they would only live and abide by the Word of God.

In the Book of Genesis, God instituted the law of seedtime and harvest. He also created the first living beings and gave them the ability and capacity to grow and multiply. Your life began by the seed principle. Every act of your life has been operated by the seed principle because your confession determines whether you produce good seeds or bad seeds. According to Proverbs 18:21 The Message version, "Words kill, words give life; they're either poison or fruit—you choose." This amazing passage clearly states that death or life in my situation is determined by the words I speak.

The majority of society is not conscious of their seed planting. The purpose of this book is to give you the steps to overcome every challenge, every situation, and every circumstance you will face in life and help you to reach your maximum potential by using God's spiritual laws of seedtime and harvest. Some of the information covered in this book will be repetitive to highlight the importance of the seed faith principles.

Dr. E.L. Womack, Sr.

Chapter 1

The Principle of the Seed

"The sower sows the Word. The ones along the path are those who have the Word sown [in their hearts], but when they hear, Satan comes at once and [by force] takes away the message which is sown in them. And in the same way the ones sown upon stony ground are those who, when they hear the Word, at once receive and accept and welcome it with joy;" **Mark 4:14–16 (AMP)**

Every seed in the natural and spiritual realm is supposed to grow. God guarantees increase from sowing His Word in your heart. The sower in Mark 4:14 represents you, the believer, and God's Word is the seed. Satan is the one who takes away the Word and will stop you from growing and developing. Satan is your enemy, and he comes to steal, kill, and destroy, according to John 10:10.

Our focus is on the seed sown along the path, which is your life's journey. When you do not understand a thing, the wicked one (Satan) comes and take away that which you have heard and sown in your heart.

Testimony: In the '80s my wife and I were believing God for $30,000 to get out of debt. It was posted on our vision board on the wall in our bedroom so we could see it every day. We prayed and agreed and confessed 1 John 5:14–15 KJV daily which states, " And this is the confidence that we have in him, that, if we ask any thing according to his will, he heareth us: And if we know that he hear us, whatsoever we ask, we know that we have the petitions that we desired of him." One day I received a call from a man of God stating another man, who lived out of town, saw me in a vision. He called the man of God in my city and asked if he knew a man that matched my description. He stated he saw me in a vision where God had answered my prayers and met all my needs and told him to call me and tell me. The man called and asked me what my present need was. I told him $3,000, which was my present need; however, our vision board showed us believing God for $30,000.

The enemy came in and had me focused on the present need instead of what I believed for on my vision board. This is exactly how the enemy will come in and take away that which was sown in your heart if you do not stay focused on your vision and path of life. When you do not understand the Word, the wicked one will come to confuse you and take the Word from you. This will cause you to come against stumbling blocks and not have a specific victory in your life.

"Listen then to what the parable of the sower means: When anyone hears the message about the kingdom and does not understand it, the evil one comes and snatches away what was sown in their heart. This is the seed sown along the path.
The seed falling among the thorns refers to someone who hears the word, but the worries of this life and the deceitfulness of wealth choke it, making it unfruitful. But the seed falling on good soil refers to someone who hears the word and understands it. This is the one who produces a crop, yielding a hundred, sixty or thirty times what was sown." Matthew 13:18–19, 22–23 (NIV)

This parable Jesus spoke helps bring revelation of the seed to life. This parable is an earthly story that gives a heavenly meaning. Matthew and Mark both speak of the Word of God as a seed that we must plant or sow into our hearts.

If the Word of God is the seed that must be sown in the heart and if we understand how the principle works, the wicked one cannot take away that which was sown in our hearts.

There are many things that will stop you from receiving the greatest blessing God has for you by choking the word you received as weeds choke the root of a seed. They include: the world's system, the cares of this world, running behind money, and allowing money to be your god. As mentioned earlier about believing God for $30,000, I had it on my vision board; I was praying and confessing, but it was not planted in my heart. I didn't believe it would actually happen. So when the opportunity presented itself for me to tell the man of God what my present need was, I choked and was deceived and missed out on my need I had believed for by stating less. I was focused on my present situation of $3,000 and that's what I received. The Word of God is the most important thing you can have in life. We must allow the Word of God to be number one in our lives. It is the seed that must be planted, and you must be determined to not allow anything to stop you from planting the seed of the Word of God. You can plant the seed of the Word of God in your heart through personal study time, listening to your pastor's and other sermons, group Bible study, or weekly church services. The Word you deliberately plant in your heart becomes a seed specific for your garden of life.

Testimony: Being in the construction industry, sometimes my work is based on the weather. Sometimes it would rain for a week or two and cause situations in my home to get behind. I knew God would supply my needs because He always had. In prayer, I would put God in remembrance of His word and tell Him what my needs were. I was not going to the bank to borrow because of circumstances. A few days later I heard a knock at the door. A member from our church brought me money. He said he had not been able to rest for the last two days because the Lord wanted him to bless me. I rejoiced because I understood that the Lord hears me every time I pray.

Every seed on the face of the earth has potential to bring forth fruit.

It will:

- grow.

- develop.

- bring increase in the natural.

- bring life from the spirit realm.

According to the 23rd verse, the good ground occurs when you **hear** and **understand** the Word. Fruit will come forth some 100 times more, 60 times more, and some 30 times more than what was planted.

You will bear fruit because you **hear, understand, and apply** the Word in your life. Understanding something means you would grasp the meaning or have, a thorough acquaintance of it. To accept as settled understanding is important because, when you understand a thing, Satan cannot take it from you. According to Proverbs 4:7 (KJV), "Wisdom is the principle thing; therefore get wisdom: and in all thy getting get understanding."

Every seed contains the ingredients to produce after its own kind. In Genesis 1:11 (KJV), God said, "Let the earth bring forth grass, the herb yielding seed, and the fruit tree yielding fruit after his kind, whose seed is in itself, upon the earth: and it was so."

In order for the seed to produce exactly what you want in life, know that there is a process. In plant biology, we learn that the seed opens in its early stage of germination. Jesus said in John 12:24 (AMP), "I assure you, most solemnly I tell you, Unless a grain of wheat falls into the earth and dies, it remains [just one grain; it never

becomes more but lives] by itself alone. But if it dies, it produces many others *and* yields a rich harvest." In the natural realm, it is easy to understand that life is in the seed. The realm of the Holy Spirit works the same way. When the seed (the Word) is planted in the earth (heart) of man, the seed will grow because there is life in the seed. The revelation is that every seed will give you an increase and a harvest in your life.

God promises that as long as there remains seasons on the earth, there will be seedtime and harvest. Genesis 8:22 (KJV) says, "While the earth remaineth, seedtime, and harvest, cold and heat, and summer and winter, and day and night shall not cease."

The harvest is promised, but the believer has to water the seed that has been planted. 1 Corinthians 3:6 (KJV) states, "I have planted, Apollos watered, but God gave the increase." What did Paul plant? The WORD. The seed is in the Word. Apollos watered the Word Paul had planted. God and His Word will give you an increase. Verse 7 states, "So then neither is he that planteth anything, neither he that watereth; but God giveth the increase." God will cause the seed to come up because that is His way of blessing the believer. That is what is called the Law of Genesis.

The word is the seed to be planted in your mind and in your heart. It is not planted until it is:

- known.

- received.

- trusted.

Keep this before you—the seed is to be planted in your heart and mind. If it is not trusted, it is not planted. It has to be planted. You must understand the system God has set up and how to water the Word. Satan cannot destroy or take the Word if you understand the principles of God's laws. When you understand this, you can put pressure on the Word by your confessions. It works the same way as when water puts pressure on the physical seed and causes it to germinate and grow.

Chapter 2

The Principle of Meditating on the Word

"This book of the law shall not depart out of thy mouth; but thou shalt meditate therein day and night, that thou mayest observe to do according to all that is written therein: for then thou shalt make thy way prosperous, and then thou shalt have good success." Joshua 1:8 (KJV)

Meditating has many meanings in the Hebrew, such as to mutter, to speak aloud, to speak under your breath, or to gaze. It is very important to meditate day and night on the Word of God because meditation helps you get the Word in your heart. When you get the Word in you, you are planting the seeds of the Word. If you plant the Word of God in your heart, you will get the harvest you are looking for in life. You will never know the Word until it is known, received, trusted, and acted upon. If you want to get the word of God planted in your heart, begin meditating, confessing, pondering, speaking the Word under your breath, and gazing at the Word.

If the Word of God is not planted in your heart, you are not going to observe the things God wants you to observe. Joshua says in verse 8 that after you have meditated day and night, you will be able to observe. To observe means to see, to sense something, to come to realization on things, and to be watchful. You will be able to watch something you have never observed before in your spiritual and natural life. The reason some people do not observe the things around them is because the seed of the Word is not planted in them.

"This is what the LORD says: 'Cursed is the one who trusts in man, who draws strength from mere flesh and whose heart turns away from the LORD. That person will be like a bush in the wastelands; they will not see prosperity when it comes. They will dwell in the parched places of the desert, in a salt land where no one lives. But blessed is the one who trust in the LORD, whose confidence is in him. They will be like a tree planted by the water that sends out its roots by the stream. It does not fear when heat comes; its leaves are always green. It has no worries in a year of drought and never fails to bear fruit." Jeremiah 17:5–8 (NIV)

To put trust in God means to put trust in His Word. When you trust God, the seed of the Word planted in your heart will cause you to both see spiritually and observe the natural things around you. Meditating on the seed of the Word will allow you to be able to see things you normally would not have seen and to do things you have never done before. You will also be able to sense when there is danger ahead. This comes through the seed of the Word of God that you have planted and watered daily. It works every time.

We have believers who are always bumping into foolishness, and we have Christian people who get tied up into worldly mess. The word is not planted in their hearts, and they are not meditating in the Word day and night, therefore they cannot observe what to do. Through meditating in the Word, every believer should be able to sense when something is wrong. When you observe to do, you should be able to sense things not going right in the spirit realm (Satan) and the natural realm (family, job, friends).

When you observe to do:

- You will know what to do when you are meditating on the Word.

- You will know where to go when the Word is working.

- You will know who to talk to. You cannot talk to everybody about your situation.

- You will know what to say. Because the seed is planted in your heart, you will know what to say in that same hour.

"My son, keep your father's command and do not forsake your mother's teaching. Bind them always on your heart; fasten them around your neck. When you walk, they will **guide** *you; when you sleep, they will* **watch over** *you; when you awake, they will* **speak to** *you."* Proverbs 6:20–22 (NIV)

What will? The Word of God will. If the Word is not planted, it is not working in you. You will not know what to do, you will not know where to go, you will not know whom to talk to, and you will not know what to say. The Word will work for you when you meditate on the Word of God.

According to Hebrews 4:12 (KJV), "For the Word of God is quick, and powerful, and sharper than any twoedged sword, piercing even to the dividing asunder of soul and spirit, and of the joints and marrow, and is a discerner of the thoughts and intents of the heart." The Word will reveal the thoughts and intents of a person. A man can be standing up talking to you, and you can see straight through him. You will be able to see a rascal before he gets to you because of your meditating in the Word of God. Remember, the seed of the Word is a living thing; it is not a dead letter. **God's Word is active, alive, and has creative power.**

There are two mental benefits of meditating. According to Proverbs 23:7a (KJV), "For as he thinketh in his heart, so is he." This means our behavior is a product of our thinking.

1. It equips us to make quality decisions, and this ensures our behavior and conduct is in line with the will of God.

2. It helps you maintain a renewed mind.

According to Romans 12:2 (AMP), "Do not be conformed to this world (this age), [fashioned after and adapted to its external, superficial customs], but be transformed (changed) by the [entire] renewal of your mind [by its new ideals and its new attitude], so that you may prove [for yourselves] what is the good and acceptable and perfect will of God, *even* the thing which is good and acceptable and perfect [in His sight for you]." In the mind adjusting process, speaking the pure Word of God is vital in being successful in this course of renewing the mind.

Chapter 3

The Principle of Retaining the Word

"As the rain and the snow come down from heaven, and do not return to it without watering the earth and making it bud and flourish, so that it yields seed for the sower and bread for the eater, so is my word that goes out from my mouth: It will not return to me empty, but will accomplish what I desire and achieve the purpose for which I sent it." Isaiah 55:10–11 (NIV)

You do not see the rain going up; you see the rain coming down. Any seed that is watered will bring forth a harvest. The harvest is whatever you are believing God for in your life. Whatever is in the earth will produce a harvest when it is watered. It will spring forth and bud, and you will be able to see the manifestation. The manifestation, a bud, will be the result of the seed when the water hits the earth and puts pressure on the seed in the ground.

In the natural realm, a farmer plants a seed into the ground because he wants to get something from the ground from his harvest. After many days the water comes upon the face of the earth and waters the seed he has planted. Eventually he will be able to see something from the seed that he planted.

Isaiah compares a natural seed with the Word of God. God says so shall my Word be—my Word is just like the seed planted in the earth. You will get what you believe God for from the seed you have sown in your heart. You will get results! The believer must learn how to plant the Word of God in their lives because the word guarantees a harvest when the Word is planted in the heart and understood by the believer.

A seed must be able to grow and develop. God's Word will grow and develop in the believer who will rise up and bring forth fruit in his or her life. Here are six important characteristics of the seed/Word of God:

1. **Indispensable:** God is saying through Isaiah that the promise and essential part are in the seed itself. The seed will produce in your life because the essential part is in the seed. In plant biology, the seed opens in its early stage of germination. In the natural realm, it is easy to understand that life is in the seed. It is the same way in the realm of the Holy Spirit. John 5:26 states, "For as the Father has life in himself, so he has granted the Son also to have life in himself." Life is the substance that is in the Word itself and will produce the harvest.

2. **Harvest Giver:** When the farmer goes out to plant the seed, the seed may look dead to him; nevertheless, there is life in

the seed itself. Likewise, there are manifestations prevailing in the Word itself. You are guaranteed a harvest because the nurtured seed has life already encoded in its DNA.

Then Jesus said, "God's kingdom is like seed thrown on a field by a man who then goes to bed and forgets about it. The seed sprouts and grows—he has no idea how it happens. The earth does it all without his help: first a green stem of grass, then a bud, then the ripened grain. When the grain is fully formed, he reaps—harvest time! Mark 4:26–29 (MSG).

Testimony: Some friends needed to sell their vehicle because they wanted to buy a piece of property but could not afford both. They asked us to buy the vehicle. We did not need another vehicle because all the kids had vehicles, but we decided to buy the vehicle for leisure traveling. When one of my sons came home from college, he saw the vehicle in the yard. He ran in the house and said, "Whose vehicle is that outside?" I said, "We just purchased that vehicle to help out some friends." My son could not believe it and began to shout. He said, "I have on my vision board the exact same color and style of that vehicle. I went and took a picture of the vehicle I wanted, put it on my vision board, and even test drove one. Daily I would confess that God would bless me with my new vehicle. I did not know where it was coming from, but for the past year I have been praying and believing for that vehicle. So you all actually were buying the vehicle for me. I gave the angels something to do, and they harkened to the word I was confessing."

This is an example of the first green stem of grass, then a bud, then the ripened grain. It took him a year to get his harvest, but he confessed the word and believed until the vehicle came. He did not get discouraged and stop believing for that particular vehicle. Instead, he continued to believe until it manifested.

3. **Life Giver:** It does not matter what other people are doing or saying; life is in God's word. For example, during a church service in the nineties, one of our elderly member's head began to lean to the side and mouth began to droop. While the service was going on, the spirit of God led me to stop the service and speak the word on healing and have the congregation pray. I bound up the spirit of strokes and death from her and loosed the healing power of the Word of God by laying on of my hands. I instructed her daughter to take her directly to the hospital. The doctor stated the member was trying to have a stroke, but something happened to stop the stroke. The answer was that there is life in God's Word. She came back to church in her right mind, and her mouth no longer drooped. The essential part was in the seed of the

Word, which gave her victory.

4. **Producer:** This is good to know! The Word of God will produce like the seed. If substance is in the seed itself, then substance is also in the Word of God. We take the Word of God and begin to confess the word. As we speak the Word, our inner ear picks the word of God up and feeds it into our hearts. In 2 Corinthians 4:13 (KJV), Paul states, "We having the same spirit of faith, according as it is written, I believed, and therefore have I spoken; we also believe, and therefore speak." Paul is saying we as believers must speak the word of God in order for the word to develop on the inside of us. You get the seed in your heart by confessing the word of God. **On a continuous basis, your tongue must become the pen of a ready writer...**Psalm 45:1 (KJV): "My heart is inditing a good matter: I speak of the things which I have made touching the king: my tongue is the pen of a ready writer."

    Psalm 103:20 (KJV): "Bless the LORD, ye his angels, that excel in strength, that do his commandments, hearkening unto the voice of his word." In our confession of speaking that Word, the angels serve as carriers of the Word. They are called ministering spirits, and they hearken to the voice of His words. This is how the process works when the Word is in your heart.

5. **Promise Retainer:** Whatever God promised, He will do it. In His Word, there is life. The Word is like a seed; it will

produce in your life. A package of seeds shows the fruit (the life) it will bear. Many seed companies post a guarantee on the package, promising that the seeds will bear the specific fruit.

Similarly, God's promises contain life. There are many born-again believers who do not believe what I am writing today. I have experienced it, and I am working it now. There is no way I could go forth in life with a family of nine and a congregation without the Word. Life is in the seed of the Word, and that Word will produce exactly as promised. No matter what the people say, no matter what you see around you, and no matter what the circumstances may seem to be in your life, God's promises are Yes and Amen. 2 Corinthians 1:20 (KJV) states, "For all the promises of God in him are yea, and in him Amen, unto the glory of God by us."

6. **Alive:** That is why life is in the Word. The breath of God is there, so there is life! Isaiah mentions in chapter 55 verse 11 that His Word will operate in the spirit realm exactly like a seed in the natural realm. You will get the fruit of what you are believing God for. It will manifest when you use the Word of God properly. In Acts 6:7, the Word of God increased, the number of disciples multiplied in Jerusalem greatly, and a great company of the priests were obedient to the faith. This is another example that proves that the Word of God is a living thing, that it is alive, and that there is a spiritual awakening in the Word of God itself once received.

It is alive and operates as a seed in the ground. The Word of God planted into the heart of the believer brings forth increase in the believer's life.

You must understand the process God has instituted in the earth. Isaiah mentions keeping the Word before you. God is saying that His Word is like a seed.

Acts 19:20 (KJV) states, "So mightily grew the Word of God and prevailed." It is moving. It is a living thing. If you plant the Word, the Word will grow, but you must be a hearer and a doer of the Word of God. James 1:22 The Message version states, "Don't fool yourself into thinking that you are a listener when you are anything but, letting the Word go in one ear and out the other. *Act* on what you hear! Those who hear and don't act are like those who glance in the mirror, walk away, and two minutes later have no idea who they are, what they look like."

When you plant the Word in your heart through your daily confession, the Word grows, and you will get an increase. It prevails. The Word will not only cause you to receive but you will be a blessing to those who are around you.

"Cultivate these things. Immerse yourself in them. The people will all see you mature right before their eyes! Keep a firm grasp on both your character and your teaching. Don't be diverted. Just keep at it. Both you and those who hear you will experience salvation."
1 Timothy 4:15–16 (MSG)

In the Word it states, *"Being born again, not of corruptible seed, but of incorruptible, by the word of God, which liveth and abideth for ever."* 1 Peter 1:23(KJV)

"Now that you've cleaned up your lives by following the truth, love one another as if your lives depended on it. Your new life is not like your old life. Your old birth came from mortal sperm; your new birth comes from God's living Word. Just think: a life conceived by God himself! That's why the prophet said, The old life is a grass life, its beauty as short-lived as wildflowers; Grass dries up, flowers droop, God's Word goes on and on forever. This is the Word that conceived the new life in you." 1 Peter 1:22–25(MSG)

The Word has to be in the heart, acted upon, and practiced daily. For example, when I rise up in the morning, I must say what the Word of God says about me and my situation. I must speak the Word, which is the incorruptible seed, over my life, and I must believe the Word of God is working for me by faith.

You will multiply daily when the Word of God is planted in your heart, and you must understand the process God has instituted in His Word. In times of chaos, you will rise up and get victory from the Word every time if you understand the process and work the process.

Every woman is impregnated by a man when he releases a seed, called a sperm, and that seed is planted in her womb at the right time of the month. The seed of conception will start developing and growing inside the woman because life is already in that seed.

After nine months, a baby comes forth. This is a law that God has set up. It is the time table for that human seed to produce.

If we plant the Word of God in our heart, according to God's timetable and according to how we plant and water the Word, we will receive an increase, and the results of using the Word will manifest in your life. The seed inside you is guaranteed to produce and deliver what you are believing for.

> **Testimony:** For each position I have had in life, I called for an increase for more money until I received what I needed. I started my career as a laborer. As I began to become a student of the Word of God, I began to discover God's promises on having abundance and no lack. In John 10:10b it states, "I have come that they might have life, and that they may have it more abundantly." God began to lead me in the right direction and gave me favor with my former boss man. I went to my former boss man and told him I was not making enough money to support my family and needed to start my own business. He blessed me with some start-up equipment and even recommended me for a few jobs. I stepped out on God's promises, and He gave me favor and a lucrative career, which gave me the ability to educate my seven children through college with no loans. Praise the Lord. God's promises are working.

Chapter 4

The Principle of Watering the Word

Watering the word will produce a harvest in your life.

It is the Word of God planted and watered that heals both the soul and the body. The Word will produce because God's Word is a seed. Any seed in the natural on the face of the earth that is planted into the dirt or soil will grow with proper watering. It is sure to produce a harvest on earth.

In the story of "Jack and the Beanstalk," Jack lived with his widowed mother. Jack's mother had him take the milk cow, the only source of the family's income, to the market to sell after the cow stopped producing milk. On the way, Jack met a man and traded the cow for bean seeds. His mother was angry when he did not bring any money back, threw the bean seeds out the window, and sent Jack to bed. The next day the seeds had begun to grow and produce. The seeds grew and grew into a gigantic beanstalk that ended in the sky.

Even though this is a fairy tale, the law is the same. Any seed on the face of the earth will produce after its kind with the right nourishment. The mother thought she was getting rid of the seeds, but when the seeds touched soil, they began to grow. The seed will grow if you do not allow the cares of the world to come in and choke them. We need to allow faith to rise up in our hearts. Every seed on the face of the earth will produce some type of harvest. Oh, yes! It will produce a harvest on the earth.

> *For with God nothing shall be impossible. And Mary said, Behold the handmaid of the Lord; be it unto me according to thy word. And the angel departed from her.* Luke 1:37–38 (KJV)

Jesus Christ came as a seed to the earth. The angel was not the seed but a carrier of the seed. When Mary said, "Be it unto me according to thy word," the seed was implanted into her womb. The Word (seed) planted was Jesus Christ of Nazareth. The Word developed in her and grew. Luke 1:80 states, "and the child grew, and waxed strong in spirit."

Show me a child who stayed a child for 20 years and did not grow and develop into an adult—something is wrong! Show me a plant that has been planted months without sprouting—something is wrong!

If you understand how God's system works and remain obedient, a harvest will be produced in your life. The farmer makes sure his ground is ready for the seed he plants, and when the farmer plants, he expects rain to come for a harvest: no rain, bad harvest. Get out of the natural realm, and get into the spiritual realm. The seed of the Word works just like a natural seed.

Before you plant the seed of the Word, you must make sure your heart is prepared.

Here is the way I personally prepare my heart to plant the Word:

1. I humble myself.

2. I repent.

3. I pull down every evil thought that has the potential to block me from receiving the Word.

Then afterwards, I am ready to receive, plant, and water the Word. Remember, if it is planted and watered, it will produce a harvest.

Remember in Isaiah 55:10–11 that the water comes to water the earth; the seed will come up and produce every time when it is watered. Water comes to bring growth to that seed, which equals increase. You are guaranteed an increase; as a matter of fact, you are guaranteed multiplied increase. Jesus is all about increase.

Jesus said the Word will produce a change in your life. Galatians 6:7 (KJV) states "Be not deceived; God is not mocked; for whatsoever a man soweth, that shall he also reap." Whatever is in the heart will come up, so we have to be mindful what we put in our heart. We have to guard our hearts because, according to Proverbs 4:23, out of it flows the issues of life.

If the seed is planted on concrete, that seed will do everything in its might to produce, but it cannot produce, because no root is there. The concrete is symbolic to a hard heart, which is why people with a hard heart cannot produce. Try throwing corn seeds on concrete, let water get on the seed, it will do everything in its might (heart) to produce, but it can't produce, because the concrete is hard. If the heart is tender, just like the soil or dirt, it will produce. As you walk down the sidewalk, look in the cracks of the concrete, and you will see dirt. I guarantee you will see some kind of grass growing because dirt was there.

The Bible states that the seed dies and will produce after its own kind. John 12:24–25 The Message version states, "Unless a grain of wheat is buried in the ground, dead to the world, it is never any more than a grain of wheat. But if it is buried, it sprouts and reproduces itself many times over. In the same way, anyone who holds on to life just as it is destroys that life. But if you let it go, reckless in your love, you'll have it forever, real and eternal."

You have to die to self and become a full student of the Word so that it can produce in your life. When we get our eyes off the Word and on the circumstances of life, it will choke out the seed and make it unproductive. It causes us to take laps in life. When you make the wrong decisions in life, you will miss out on opportunities. And in life, some opportunities will not come again or may take a season to present itself again.

Even the seed of a weed reproduces. When you do not understand a thing, the devil (your enemy) will come and take away the Word.

> **Testimony:** When the Word of God is planted, watered, and steadfastly trusted (firmly fixed in place, firm in belief), it will heal both soul and body. But the seed must remain planted and kept watered

before it can produce a harvest. When my daughters were in the hospital, I was told by the doctors they needed to have surgery. Immediately, I asked the doctors if they had seen miracles happen. They replied that they believed miracles happened back then but that God uses doctors now. I told them that God does use doctors, but God was going to perform a miracle, and I would have to pray about the situation. The first thing I did was go to the Word of God and write down healing scriptures, which represented my seed. Then I watered the Word of God by praying and confessing the healing scriptures three times a day. I knew in my heart that Isaiah 55:11 (MSG) was working for me. It states, "So will the words that come out of my mouth not come back empty-handed. They'll do the work I sent them to do; they'll complete the assignment I gave them." As I began to confess the healing scriptures daily, the Word began to grow in my heart. As I confessed and heard the Word, it began to do three things in me: 1. Grow in me; 2. Develop my faith; and 3. Increase my confidence in its ability to produce.

I went back to the doctors, and they wanted to take custody of my daughters to go ahead with the surgery. I told them to continue with testing as I continued to speak and water the Word daily regardless of the negative report. Friends began to tell me to get out of the way of the doctors and let them do what was best for my daughters. I did not let the cares of this world, my emotions, or any fear of doubt come into my heart. God said the seed will produce after its own kind, and I believed that. I refused to give up on God's promises. The first week an examination was done. The second week another examination was done at another hospital. The third week the examination showed nothing. A healing took place, and my daughters were able to come home. Hallelujah!

In this situation, the soil represented my heart, and the seed was the healing scriptures of the Word of God. The watering of the word took place when I confessed the healing scriptures three times a day. The seed began to germinate and bring more life and confidence to me in the Word of God supernaturally. I stayed with God's promises by not being distracted by the doctor's negative reports, friends, and emotions, so Satan could not come and take my daughters from me. I knew the harvest had come when the doctors gave me a good report. This shows that there is life in the seed of the Word of God and that watering it and trusting God's process works just as with a natural seed.

Chapter 5

The Principle of the Seed at Work

Until you receive the manifestation of what you are believing for, there are **five** things that you should be doing:

1. Refuse to become discouraged.

No matter what happens in your life, do not allow discouragement to come. You will get an increase if you keep watering the seed (speaking the Word). It may seem hard on the flesh, but stay the course. Your flesh will want to go back to the unregenerate man by cursing, fussing, drawing up in a corner, etc.

Hold your fist up and tell Satan, "I will not get discouraged. It does not matter what you try to do to me. I rebuke you, in the name of Jesus. The seed has been planted and firmly fixed in my heart. So no matter what you try to put on my family, that seed of the Word has been planted. The seed of the Word of God is working mightily in me. I will receive my harvest."

Make sure you understand this principle because the cares of the world will come to choke the seed to prevent the manifestation from happening. Refuse to allow discouragement to come by confessing and speaking God's Word only.

2. Be determined to keep your faith alive and active.

You have to keep speaking the Word and saying what God says about you. In a difficult situation, you must understand that the seed is in itself to produce after its own kind. Refuse to let anything stop your faith from being active. In hard times, you must understand how God's principles work and keep the faith. Jesus said that the Word of God is a seed, which must be planted in the heart of man and watered down daily. Remember, Paul said "I planted, Apollos watered; but God gave the increase." This was demonstration of God giving the increase when the seed was planted and then watered.

Why should you keep a positive attitude? Because you understand the principle found in Philippians 4:19 (AMP): "And my God will liberally supply (fill to the full) your every need according to His riches in glory in Christ Jesus." Believe that the situation is turning around for your good. The seed is ready to germinate. The fruit—what you are believing God for—is getting ready to manifest.

Let's consider Abraham, the father of many nations.

"Abraham didn't focus on his own impotence and say, 'It's hopeless. This hundred-year-old body could never father a child.' Nor did he survey Sarah's decades of infertility and give up. He didn't tiptoe around God's promise asking cautiously skeptical questions. He plunged into the promise and came up strong, ready for God, sure that God would make good on what he had said. That's why it is said, 'Abraham was declared fit before God by trusting God to set him right.' But it's not just Abraham; it's also us! The same thing gets said about us when we embrace and believe the One who brought Jesus to life when the conditions were equally hopeless. The sacrificed Jesus made us fit for God, set us right with God. Romans 4:19–25 (MSG)*

3. Give and keep on giving.

Stand on Luke 6:38 (NKJV): "Give, and it will be given to you: good measure, pressed down, shaken together, and running over will be put into your bosom. For with the same measure that you use, it will be measured back to you."

There are many things you can give. Start giving things away that you like, not things you do not like. You can give your precious time to someone who is lonely. If the devil tries to hinder your finances, find someone to bless financially. Love and keep loving. Find something to give away. Give your nice purse away. How about that hat you like? Men, give away your Kenneth Cole or Stacy Adams shoes, your watch, or your belt. You can cut somebody's grass. Keep on giving, give more to your ministry above tithes, keep loving, and keep helping! Help somebody because you know the seed is germinating and getting ready to manifest for you.

4. Be assured of your guaranteed harvest.

This is the step where your faith in God's Word kicks in. In 1 John 5:14–15 AMP it states, "And this is the confidence (the assurance, the privilege of boldness) which we have in Him: [we are sure] that if we ask anything (make any request) according to His will (in agreement with His own plan), He listens to *and* hears us. And if (since) we [positively] know that He listens to us in whatever we ask, we also know [with settled and absolute knowledge] that we have [granted us as our present possessions] the requests made of Him."

You have to become excited at this point because Genesis 8:22 (KJV) states, "While the earth remaineth, seedtime and harvest, and cold and heat, and summer and winter, and day and night shall not cease. "This is a vital process that the entire Word of God is based on, and that is the Law of Reciprocity. This divine reciprocity demands two things:

- If you plant a seed, the ground will give you a harvest.

- The ground can only give back to you as you give to the ground.

For an example, in the book of Genesis, Isaac sowed in the time of a famine, and he received a hundred times what he sowed.

> *"...Giving, not getting, is the way. Generosity begets generosity."* Luke 6:38 (MSG)

5. Continue in an attitude of expectation, and work the Word.

Keep your expectancy up because you understand that the process of the seed producing is guaranteed. God cannot lie. Do not give up! Do not back up! We are not of them that draw back to perdition. The Word of God states if you understand a thing, the devil cannot take it. If you throw your hands up and say this process does not work, the devil has come in and choked the Word that was sown in you.

Keep rejoicing when things seem to get worse because everything is subject to change. Stick to what God has said. Hold on to the seed of the Word. Stop letting the devil steal from you. Stay on the Word, and refuse to allow discouragement to come. Whatever gesture you use to help you reinforce your confession, do it to emphasize your belief. It can be shaking your head, raising your fist up, and saying, "I will not accept discouragement."

Guard your heart daily with the Word of God, not foolishness. If the wrong thing is planted in your garden (heart), in your home, or on your job, it's going to bring forth a different kind of harvest that you are not looking for.

If I had known earlier how important the Word of God was, I would have required my children to memorize the book of Proverbs when they were very young. The seed would have been in them and would come up in a time of need. However, once I understood how important it was to have the Word grow inside of them, I would have my children confess Charles Capps' confessions on our way to school and even while we were vacationing.

I constantly maintain an attitude of expectancy. I am looking for someone to come up to me and write me out a check for thousands of dollars. It has happened before; it will happen again. I constantly tell my children that the favor of God is upon them because God has crowned us with favor.

> *"Let not mercy and truth forsake thee: bind them around thy neck; write them upon the table of thine heart: So shalt thou find favour and good understanding in the sight of God and man."* Proverbs 3:3–4 (KJV)

Put the Word in at the proper time, according to Isaiah 55:11. The Word of God will prosper you. God is a God of increase. If you stick with the Word, it will give you increase. The lying devil will try to get you to go another direction in life, besides God's way, but please, child of God, stick with the Word. Do not take the Word and throw it out the window. In the book of Proverbs, it states there is a way that seems right to man but the end there of are the ways of destruction.

The Word of God brings deliverance in your life. On your job, when you are being overlooked or overloaded, say kind words. The devil wants you to get in the flesh, but know that the seed of the Word is working mightily in you. Know that the seed of the Word is working mightily in you. The Word of God is a seed.

Chapter 6

The Principle of God's Ability in the Word

This is good! This is what blesses me! When you speak, mutter, and meditate on God's Word, the creative ability of God's Word is developed inside your heart. You can face anything that the devil tries to throw at you and your family because of your meditating on the Word day and night. It causes you to see in ways you have never seen before. You begin to have God's ability, not your own. Not boasting in myself, the Word is working for me; it will also work for you.

With this ability in God, I can see why no prophet went out on his own; only false prophets did. Every prophet from God went out on the ability of the Word of God because, before they went out, they were instructed by God to eat the Word. Proverbs 6:22 speaks about the Word guiding you, watching over you, and speaking to you. Now we can see that this ability that's working in them is able to do exceedingly, abundantly above all that they may ask or think according to the power that worketh in them.

The things God wants to do for you must be conceived in your spirit before they can become a reality in your life. Joshua reminds us, that after you observe to do, according to all that is written therein, you will make your way prosperous. Can you see it now? Every prophet made his way prosperous because the seed of the Word was planted in him.

The enemy messes with the mind of the believer if he is not meditating on the Word concerning everyday life. The Bible states that you will make your way prosperous (bind the devil) through the process of the seed of the Word being planted in your heart. By being a hearer and doer of the Word, you are activating a few other things to happen in the process. You are doing the work, the Word is working through you, and God is working through the Word by His spirit. So, therefore, you are making your way prosperous.

God created us with two sets of ears: the outer ear and the inner ear. The outer ear is what you see, and the inner ear is made up of bone structure. The inner ear feeds the words you hear directly into your spirit. For example, that is why He told Joshua to keep the Word of God before him day and night because the inner ear feeds your voice directly to the human spirit. That is why what you say will affect you more than what somebody else says. What you say, you hear, and your inner ear feeds your voice directly into your human spirit.

The Word begins to grow, and whatever you are saying all the time will begin to grow on the inside as well as develop on the inside. This is important; the inner ear feeds your voice directly into your human spirit, which is called the heart. **What you say affects you more than what your neighbor states about you.**

The science of medicine states that they have discovered

parts of the brain that are connected to the human speech and to every nerve in the body. So this means the words you speak will affect your entire life. When you continue to speak the same things on a regular basis, whether positive or negative, they will be planted in your heart. In our lives, we are spirit beings; this is how God designed us in order that the Word can go right into our human recreated spirits. When we get the Word in our human spirit, the Word of God begins to grow on the inside.

As I was meditating and seeking God, He revealed to me the importance of speaking the Word of God daily in my life so that it can get into my heart. The Word will produce fruit in my life. I want you to understand that the inner ear feeds your confession of God's Word directly into your human (recreated) spirit, which is referred to as the heart of the human spirit. The Word of God takes up residence in you, and it will affect your entire being.

Have you ever noticed people who are always cussing or fighting? It is in their hearts. There are born again believers and church goers who are not being **hearers** and **doers** of the Word of God. They have been saying the wrong thing. The inner ear has taken their negative words and fed it into their spirit. Negative words and not the Word have grown into their spirit.

The only way to get negative words out is to let the seed of the Word take the negative word's place. Once there, the Word of God will then uproot, tear down, destroy, and overthrow the negativity and begin to build and to plant what is needed to clean up, grow, and develop you in the things of God.

Many Christians refuse to take the time to put the Word in their heart. They refuse to meditate day and night and confess God's Word daily. Be sure that you are meditating and pondering on the Word of God. There are many opportunities you can use to speak the Word aloud over your circumstances. Try making it a practice to do it on your way to work, on your lunch break, and before you go to bed.

A good example is my wife's mother, who had fifteen children. Every morning after the children were gone to school, she would go in the restroom with her Bible and Sunday school book.

The Word of God must be planted in the heart of every believer. This will change your life, you will be able to observe, sense, see, and be watchful of your surroundings because the Word is developing you on the inside.

- **Through meditating, the creative ability of God is developing in your heart.**

- **The things that you want God to do must be conceived in your spirit or in your heart before it becomes a reality in your life.**

Have you ever started doing something for God physically or spiritually and stopped? You said you were going to pray an hour every day, started off well, then stopped. You have to declare war; speak what you want to do, and say, "I am going to accomplish getting the Word in my heart." The desire comes from the inside. Then you can go forward in life. Many today start out but fall back because they stop speaking God's word.

"My heart was hot within me. While I was musing, the fire burned; then spoke I with my tongue." Psalm 39:3 (AMP)

"Is not My word like fire [that consumes all that cannot endure the test]? says the Lord, and like a hammer that breaks in pieces the rock [of most stubborn resistance]?" Jeremiah 23:29 (AMP)

In Psalm 39, David writes, "while I was musing." Musing means meditating and speaking in the Hebrew. As I was mediating in the Word, my heart was hot within me and I began to speak out. David said, "I opened my mouth, and I began to speak because I felt a burning on the inside." He is speaking of meditating on God's Word. This is a good example of the seed of the Word being so powerful that at times it is too strong to keep it to ourselves. For example, if the teacher asks a question and you know the answer, she says raise your hand. It takes every ounce of discipline in you to hold your tongue until you are called on. What happens when you meditate day and night? In Jeremiah, God declares His Word to be like a fire and like a hammer that breaks a rock in pieces (circumstances in pieces).

> **Testimony:** The same thing happens at times when I get up to speak. I feel a heat within me. This does not happen all the time. I believe certain messages are needed for that hour. When I meditate on the Word for a whole week and then get around people, it's hard to hold the Word within me. I have to tell

somebody. The Word brings an excitement on the inside because it is a living thing.

In Luke 24, Jesus had ministered to the disciples. The disciples said in verse 32, "Did not our hearts burn within us, while He talked with us by the way, and while he opened to us the scriptures?" The Word felt like it was burning on the inside because the Word is alive. Do not allow circumstances to move you. Rise up and speak the Word conceived in your heart. The Word works.

Every minister of the gospel should have a Word from the Lord that will burn the ears of the people. When we learn the principle and the process of getting the Word in our hearts and training our human spirits, nothing shall be able to move us from the hope of the Lord Jesus Christ. You can train your spirit just like you train your children.

Now, I can see in the book of Proverbs why David put so much emphasis on putting the Word in your heart. In Proverbs 3:3 (KJV) it states, "Let not mercy and truth forsake thee: bind them about thy neck; write them on the table of thine heart." It is something about the heart. What is it about the heart? The heart is the dirt (ground, soil) where the seed of the Word of God must be planted. The farmer uses the heart of the earth, the dirt, to plant the seed. God's Word to us must be conceived in our heart in order for us to get the reality of the things we desire in life. Your spiritual development relies on you getting the Word of God into your heart.

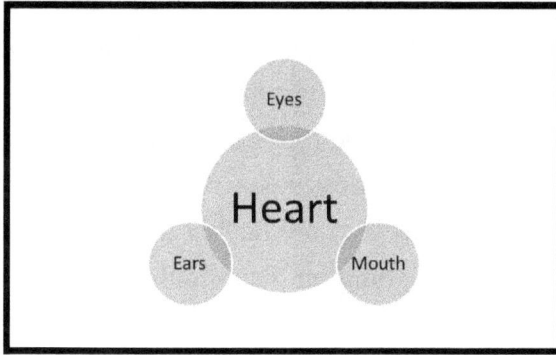

Proverbs 4 speaks about attending to the Word, inclining your ears to the Word, looking at the Word, and Maintaining the Word within your heart.

He is showing how important the Word is. The Word will grow and develop on the inside you so that you can get a harvest. Then you will be able to observe all the things around you, both spiritual and natural. Remember, you will know where to go, and when you get there, you will know what to say because of the Word of God working on the inside of you. Look what the scripture states —let your heart retain my words; keep my commandments and live. David continues to ponder the Word to the body of Christ.

"My son, keep my words; lay up within you my commandments [for use when needed] and treasure them. Keep my commandments and live, and keep my law and teaching as the apple (the pupil) of your eye. Proverbs 7:1–2 (AMP)

He is trying to get us to see the process that God has set up whereby the Word must be put in the heart. You are not living until you get the Word of God in you and until you get the full manifestation of fruit in your life. This happens through continued spiritual growth and development. We see people who look good on the outside, and we think they are having a good time just enjoying themselves and have it going on—but hold it! You have not started living until you get the Word of God in your heart. Our church passes out a daily reading calendar each month to encourage the body of Christ to put the Word in their heart.

"But mark this: There will be terrible times in the last days. People will be lovers of themselves, lovers of money, boastful, proud, abusive, disobedient to their parents, ungrateful, unholy, without love, unforgiving, slanderous, without self-control, brutal, not lovers of the good, treacherous, rash, conceited, lovers of pleasure rather than lovers of God—" 2 Timothy 3:1–4 (NIV)

We can see now the fulfillment of scriptures. The perilous dangerous times are here. This is why David says you need to get the Word in your heart so you can be able to sustain (hold up, keep from falling) from what is coming upon the earth. Parents, if you know what is getting ready to happen upon the face of the earth, do like David did for his son Solomon (wisest man on the earth) and teach them God's Word and how to apply the Word in their lives. If you do not teach them God's Word, your children will fall for the foolishness that is coming up on the earth, and they will miss heaven.

Solomon says bind them (restrain) them about thy neck and write them upon the table of thine heart. Joshua says this book of the law shall not depart from out of my mouth. He also states that the way you get it into the heart is by meditating and speaking it; your inner ear will pick it up and feed it into your spirit.

You could be riding down the street and the Word is working on the inside of you. Once again, when the Word is planted in the heart, you are getting the ability of God developing on the inside of you. It must be conceived in you before it can become a reality in your life.

You can be eating your lunch and muttering the Word; people will begin to watch and wonder what you are saying. When you are riding down the street, the Word will began to talk to you (it is a spirit) because it is alive.

"Moreover he said unto me, Son of man, eat that thou findest; eat this roll and, go speak unto the house of Israel. So I opened my mouth, and he caused me to eat that roll. And he said unto me, Son of man, cause thy belly to eat, and fill thy bowels with this roll that I give thee. Then did I eat it; and it was in my mouth as honey for sweetness." Ezekiel 3:1–3 (KJV)

The words belly and bowels are symbolic to the heart and spirit of man. He is saying to put the Word of God in the inner man. Ezekiel had to get it in his mouth first in order for the Word to get into his heart. He had to speak it aloud and meditate on it, and then the Word grew in him. The Bible states he went forth and prophesied to the house of Israel and began to speak God's Word. The key to getting it in the heart is that your tongue must become the pen of a ready writer (Psalm 45:1c). Write the Word in your heart by speaking it and meditating on it day and night. Then the Word will work for you. The more you speak the Word, the more it will grow and becomes alive in you, enabling it to produce a harvest in your life.

Conclusion

It is clearly stated in each chapter that God's Word is the seed. In order to have the success that the Bible speaks about, the Body of Christ must understand the Word as a seed and how it can be used to activate their faith. As you read this book, you will notice several principles are repeated constantly for clarity and understanding. **Learning takes place with frequent repetition.**

The entire effort for writing this book is because God spoke to my spirit and said to put this information in a book. It is my heart's desire to bring understanding to the body of Christ about the process of the Word of God working in the lives of the believers. The order of this process is mention in Mark 4:26–29, where The Message version states, "Then Jesus said, 'God's kingdom is like seed thrown on a field by a man who then goes to bed and forgets about it. The seed sprouts and grows—he has no idea how it happens. The earth does it all without his help: first a green stem of grass, then a bud, then the ripened grain. When the grain is fully formed, he reaps—harvest time!"

Please remember the steps to your harvest:

1. The seed of the Word first must be in your mouth; this will not only allow you to speak it but to hear it.
2. After confessing and hearing the Word, this will allow the word to get into your heart.
3. Once it is in your heart, it will begin to develop and grow.

4. Once developed and grown, the harvest is sure.

I hope this book will encourage you and provide a spark or ignite your faith in life's situations to live the maximized life that God has intended for you.

Mark 11:23 (KJV) states, "For verily I say unto you, That whosoever shall say unto this mountain, Be thou removed, and be thou cast into the sea; and shall not doubt in his heart, but shall believe that those things which he saith shall come to pass; he shall have whatsoever he saith."

Prayer for Salvation

Heavenly Father,

You said in Your Word that whosoever shall call upon the name of the Lord shall be saved, so I am calling on Jesus right now. Lord, I confess and acknowledge You with my mouth that Jesus is Lord, and in my heart, I believe and trust that You raised Him from the dead. I accept You and confess You as my Lord and Savior. Thank You, Father, for forgiving me, adopting me as Your child, and making me a new creature altogether in Christ Jesus. Amen.

If you have prayed this prayer to receive Jesus Christ as your Lord and Savior for the first time, please feel free to contact us by e-mail for prayer at believersfaithfellowship@yahoo.com or write to us at:
Believers Faith Fellowship Church
Dr. E.L. Womack, Sr.
3965 East Brookstown Drive
Baton Rouge, LA 70805
www.bffministries.org

John 1:1 "In the beginning was the Word…"

About Dr. E.L. Womack, Sr.

Dr. E.L. Womack, Sr. was born and raised in Mobile, Alabama. He was drafted into the United States Army after high school and became a sergeant within fourteen months of entering the military. As a result of his combat in the Vietnam War, he earned a Purple Heart and many other metals. He is currently an entrepreneur and enjoys real estate investments.

After knowing his wife for only three months, on September 18, 1970, Dr. Womack and Audrey Womack were joined in unity. They are the proud parents of seven children. Now, 44 years later, the Lord continually strengthens them as they submit to each other.

Dr. Womack attended Rhema Word of Faith School in 1981. He was licensed in 1982 and ordained in 1983 by the National Baptist Association under the late Reverend John D. Lands of Gloryland Baptist Church in Baton Rouge, Louisiana. Dr. Womack, who is a certified Christian Counselor, was honored with a doctorate of divinity from E.L. White Seminary School in Mobile, Alabama. He is also the founder of God Comfort Ministerial Alliance, Inc.

Early in his ministry, God deeply impressed Dr. Womack to teach the body of Christ "how to walk by faith." He started a Bible study in his home, and this humble beginning became Believers Faith Fellowship Church in 1985. His ministry has impacted the lives of many ministers and pastors in the city of Baton Rouge.

Dr. Womack is a member of the Association of Independent Ministries under the direction of Drs. I.V. and Bridget Hilliard of Houston, Texas. He is also an active member of MOVE under the leadership of Pastor Adam Richardson, Sr.

He believes in the operation of the nine gifts of the Holy Spirit and teaching the uncompromised Word of God.

Seed-Based Confessions for Overcoming Life's Challenges

In order for the Word of God to be planted in your heart, you have to make sure your heart is changed by your confession of Jesus Christ through salvation.

<u>Healing</u>

I am healed by the stripes of Jesus, and His healing power is flowing through my body.
Isaiah 53:5

Because Jesus took my infirmities and bore my sickness, I am healed.
He forgives all my iniquities and heals all my diseases.
Matthew 8:17

I am the righteousness of God in Christ and by His stripes I am healed.
1Peter 2:24

<u>Prosperity</u>

I am prospering and in perfect health as my soul prospers.
3John 2

I have gone through challenging times, but the Word continues to bring me out to a wealthy place.
Psalm 66:12

I will always seek the Lord, and He will prosper me.
2 Chronicles 26:5

I do not walk in lack of any kind because my house is filled with plenty and my God supplies all my needs according to His riches in Glory by Christ Jesus.
Philippians 4:19, Proverbs 3:10

Favor
I find favor and good understanding with God and everyone I come in contact with.
Proverbs 3:4

My enemies do not triumph over me, because the Lord has favored me.
Psalm 47:11

I am a cheerful giver, and God has made all grace abound toward me.
2 Corinthians 9:7-8

Faith
I am whole and of good comfort because of my faith in God's Word.

All things are possible for me because I believe and apply and walk in God's Word.
Matthew 9:22

Because I do not doubt, I will receive everything I believe for in God's Word.
James 1:6

Daily, I walk by faith and in God's Word and not by what I see.
2 Corinthians 5:7

<u>Fear and Worry</u>
I overcome evil with good.
Romans 12:21

I am an overcomer because the Greater One lives on the inside of me.
John 4:4

I don't walk in fear, because God has given me power, love, and a sound mind.
2 Timothy 1:7

I will not worry or have any anxiety, because the Word is working mightily in me.
Philippians 4:6

Peace

I walk in peace because of the strength of God's Word.
Psalm 29:11

I keep my heart and mind in perfect peace because my mind stays on the Word of God.
Isaiah 26:3

I am spiritually minded, and it brings me life and peace.
Romans 8:6

I let the peace of God rule in my heart, and I refuse to worry.
Colossians 3:15

Wisdom and Direction

Daily, I walk in the wisdom and knowledge of God's Word, which causes me to make quality decisions.
John 16:13, James 1:5

Every day of my life my spiritual eyes are open, and I am enlightened with understanding.
Ephesians 1:18

I acknowledge the Lord, and He will direct me in the right ways to go.
Proverbs 3:6

The Word of God lives in me and teaches me all things.
John 15:7